AF255477

Little Princess

Easy Bake Oven Cookbook

365-Days Easy & Amazing Easy Bake Oven Recipes for Girls

Tabatha Pincus

Table of Contents

Note to Parents or Guardians... 5

What is the Easy-Bake Ultimate Oven? 6

Tips for Baking With Kids.. 7

Using the Easy-Bake Ultimate Oven—The Basics 7

Snacks 9

Cinnamon Crisp 9
Bean Dip Nachos...10
Baked Cinnamon Apple 11
Scones...12
Marshmallow Mud 13
Peanut Butter Fudge...14
Rice Krispies Treats 15
Popcorn Balls..16
Chocolate Covered Pretzels 17
Bacon Roll-Ups 18
Cheese Balls..19
Cinnamon Bread Pudding 20

Cookies and Biscuits 21

Cheesy Biscuits...21
Almond Cookies 22
Snowball Cookies 23
Sugar Cookies 24
Oatmeal Cookies 25
Pecan Cookies 26
Potato Drop Cookies 27
Rosemary Biscuits 28
Chocolate and Oatmeal Cookies 29
Snow Mound Cookies 30
Princess Cookies 31
Chocolate Chip Cookies 32
Angel Food Cake Mix Cookies.............................33

Cakes 34

Banana Cream Cake 34
Cornbread 35
Pretty Pink Cake 36
Lemon Cake 37
Tea Cake..38

Peanut Butter Cake 39

Toffee Trifle Cake 40

Red Velvet Cake...41

Vanilla Cake 42

Chocolate Birthday Cake 43

Chocolate Lava Cake 44

Easy Baked Alaska 45

Pretty Rose Cake...46

Party Cake 47

Brownies and Bars 48

Little Prince Bars (With Dulce de Leche) 48

Baby Brownies 49

Six Layer Bars 50

Apple Bar 51

Orange Marmalade Bars...52

Easy-Bake Oven Brownies 53

Chocolate Milk Brownies..54

Granola Bars 55

Chocolate Coconut Bars 56

Chocolate Peanut Butter Bar 57

Oatmeal Fruit Bar..58

Fudge Brownies 59

Peanut Butter Butterscotch Brownie 60

Pizzas, Pies, and Other Savory Delights 61

Lasagna 61

Cheesy Bagel...62

Cheese and Pepperoni Muffins 63

Apple Pie...64

Blueberry Pie 65

Cherry Pie 66

Banana Split 67

Cheese Sauce/Dip 67

Asian Peanut Sauce 68

Beef and Tater Tot Casserole 69

Cheese Pizza 70

Cheese Quesadilla 71

Caramel Apple Tart 72

Conclusion 73

Before children start using the Easy-Bake Ultimate Oven for baking, the supervising parent/guardian needs to remember that:

- Hands should be washed before making food.
- The oven should never be immersed in water.
- The oven should be resting on a flat, level surface when in use.
- The baking pan and baking tool should be hand washed and dried before use.
- The pan tool should be used when pushing the pan through the oven.
- The oven must be turned off and unplugged when not in use.
- An adult should carefully handle all warm/hot pans and food during or after cooking.
- The oven, pan, and food should be allowed to cool before handling.
- Supervision by adults is needed when children are cooking. Children should not be allowed to touch the oven when items are being prepared in it.
- An adult should check that the metal doors are closed when the oven is preheating and cooking.

- Adults must give timely reminders to children about what parts of the oven are safe to touch and which parts can hurt them.
- Children should be told what kitchen tasks are for grown-ups only and which are for kids.
- Children should be given some basic rules regarding using the oven. For example, do not touch the baking pan once it is taken out of the oven and always wash their hands.

Never:
- Leave an empty pan or tool inside the oven.
- Use the oven near water.
- Leave the oven plugged in when unattended.
- Put your fingers inside the oven.

What is the Easy-Bake Ultimate Oven?

For any child interested in baking and cooking, the Easy-Bake Ultimate Oven is a dream come true. The oven uses a heating element similar to a conventional oven to cook food. The appliance has a large cooking chamber where the food is cooked in the baking pan. On the other end is the cooling chamber, where the food is left to cool for five minutes before being pushed out of the oven. The Easy-Bake Ultimate Oven makes baking and cooking for children safe, accessible, fun, and easy.

The Easy-Bake Ultimate Oven isn't just a child-friendly kitchen appliance. It creates a fantastic cooking experience where children can learn and develop some basic cooking techniques. It's also a great way to share some quality time with a parent or guardian.

This cookbook helps children learn and practice measuring ingredients and reading recipe directions while using the Easy-Bake Oven. They'll become familiar with different ingredients and utensils and learn how to work safely around the kitchen.

The Easy-Bake phenomenon isn't a fad. For years kids have been using this oven for cooking truly delicious recipes. Its fame and appeal endure for both girls and boys. Kids love this fun and easy-to-use appliance that bakes food they've prepared right in front of their eyes. It's the perfect gift for children aged eight years and over.

The Easy-Bake Ultimate Oven lets kids cook some of the foods that their parents make in a regular oven. This includes pizza, cake, cookies, and brownies.

The Easy-Bake Ultimate Oven comes with:
- Pan tool (pan pusher on one end, spatula on the other)
- Baking pan
- Instructions

- Set basic rules for baking and using utensils in the kitchen.
- Baking is an excellent way to bond with kids, so appreciate and encourage their efforts. You'll be creating wonderful memories while helping them learn new things.
- Provide clear instructions before they start baking. This includes making them understand which tool is used for what specific task.
- Let them explore a variety of ingredients.
- Select an appropriate recipe for something that they'll enjoy making.
- Planning is crucial. Ensure you have all the necessary ingredients and lay them out. Talk to them about the recipe before starting the preparation and cooking process.
- Teach them about basic kitchen hygiene.
- Allow them to touch and taste the food they've baked.

Using the Easy-Bake Ultimate Oven—The Basics

Each time you help a child use the Easy-Bake Ultimate Oven, you'll need to go through the following steps:

1. Plug the oven in and turn it on.
2. Preheat the oven for 20 minutes.
3. Spray the baking pan with cooking spray.
4. Prepare the food mix as per the recipe instructions.
5. Put your prepared food in the prepared baking pan. Ensure that any batter/mix is only up to the pan's fill line and not higher than the edge of the pan. Flatten if it's too high.
6. Place the baking pan into the baking slot.
7. Use the pan tool to push the baking pan into the baking chamber. Stop when the baking line on the tool's handle lines up with the edge of the baking slot.
8. Look inside the oven to make sure that the metal doors are closed on both sides.
9. Cook for the time given as per the recipe instructions.
10. When cooking time is over, use the pan tool to push the pan all the way through to the cooling chamber. Let it cool for 5 minutes. Make sure that you don't leave the pan tool inside the oven.
11. Use the pan tool to slide the baking pan out of the oven.
12. Turn off the oven.

Please note that for ALL of the recipes in this book:

- The oven must be preheated for 20 minutes before cooking.
- The baking pan must be sprayed with cooking spray before anything is added to it.
- You may need to cook a recipe in batches.
- Keep an eye on food while it's being cooked; sometimes, it may need to be baked for shorter or longer periods of time. The times given in these recipes are just a guide.
- After cooking, the pan must be pushed into the cooling chamber for 5 minutes before being taken out of the oven.

We hope you and your child enjoy making these scrumptious recipes!

Cinnamon Crisp

Prep Time: 10 minutes

Cook Time: 20 minutes

Serves: 2

Ingredients

- 1 cup flour
- ½ teaspoon salt
- 6 teaspoons shortening
- 2 tablespoons ice water
- Pinch of cinnamon
- Pinch of sugar

Directions

1. Combine the flour and shortening in a bowl.

2. Add the water and stir to make a dough.

3. Roll the dough out on a lightly floured flat surface.

4. Sprinkle the top of the dough with the cinnamon, salt, and sugar.

5. Cut into shapes. Triangles work well.

6. Put the shapes onto the prepared baking pan.

7. Bake in the oven until the crisp turns brown, about 20 minutes.

Serving Suggestion: Serve with jelly.

Variation Tip: None—this recipe is perfect as it is!

Nutritional Information per Serving:

Calories 342 | Fat 13.4g | Sodium 583mg | Carbs 0g | Fiber 1.8g | Sugar 0.4g | Protein 6.5g

Bean Dip Nachos

Prep Time: 10 minutes

Cook Time: 10 minutes

Serves: 2

Ingredients

- 1 cup tortilla chips
- 1 tablespoon bean dip
- 2 tablespoons cheese, grated

Directions

1. Spread the tortilla chips out on the prepared baking pan.

2. Top with the bean dip, then the grated cheese.

3. Put the pan inside the oven and bake until the cheese melts, about 10 minutes.

Serving Suggestion: Serve with salsa and guacamole.

Variation Tip: You can use any type of cheese you prefer.

Nutritional Information per Serving:

Calories 232 | Fat 12.3g |Sodium 138mg | Carbs 23g | Fiber 3g | Sugar 0.1g | Protein 7.5g

Baked Cinnamon Apple

Prep Time: 10 minutes

Cook Time: 22 minutes

Serves: 1

Ingredients

- 1 large apple
- ¼ teaspoon butter, melted
- ⅛ teaspoon ground cinnamon
- 1 tablespoon sugar, melted

Directions

1. Wash the apple, then remove its core.

2. Slice across the apple to make thick rings.

3. Put the apple slices in the prepared baking pan.

4. Sprinkle the cinnamon and sugar on top of the apple slices.

5. Put the butter on top.

6. Bake in the oven for about 19–22 minutes.

7. Serve and enjoy!

Serving Suggestion: Serve topped with caramel syrup and chopped nuts.

Variation Tip: Use margarine instead of butter.

Nutritional Information per Serving:

Calories 175 | Fat 1.9g | Sodium 9mg | Carbs 43g | Fiber 5.6g | Sugar 35.5g | Protein 0.5g

Scones

Prep Time: 15 minutes

Cook Time: 18 minutes

Serves: 2

Ingredients

- 1 tablespoon sour cream
- $\frac{1}{8}$ teaspoon baking soda
- $\frac{1}{3}$ cup all-purpose flour
- 1 tablespoon sugar
- $\frac{1}{8}$ teaspoon baking powder
- $\frac{1}{8}$ teaspoon cream of tartar
- $\frac{1}{8}$ teaspoon salt
- 1 tablespoon butter
- 1 tablespoon raisins (optional)

Directions

1. Whisk together the sour cream and baking soda in a small bowl with a hand mixer, and then set aside.

2. Combine the flour, baking powder, sugar, cream of tartar, and salt in a mixing bowl.

3. Add in the butter, raisins, and sour cream mixture and make a dough

4. Knead the prepared dough on a floured surface.

5. Roll the dough out to ½-inch thick.

6. Cut the dough into rounds and place them on the prepared baking pan.

7. Bake in the oven for 18 minutes.

Serving Suggestion: Serve with jelly.

Variation Tip: Use margarine instead of butter.

Nutritional Information per Serving:

Calories 176 | Fat 7.2g | Sodium 272mg | Carbs 26g | Fiber 0.7g | Sugar 8.8g | Protein 2.5g

Marshmallow Mud

Prep Time: 10 minutes

Cook Time: 5 minutes

Serves: 2

Ingredients

- ¼ cup rice cereal
- 5 small marshmallows
- 2 tablespoons chocolate chips

Directions

1. Put the cereal in the prepared baking pan.

2. Put the chocolate chips over the cereal.

3. Add the marshmallows.

4. Press the mixture down a bit

5. Put the pan in the oven and bake for 5 minutes.

6. Enjoy!

Serving Suggestion: Serve with a drizzle of chocolate syrup on top.

Variation Tip: You can add some chopped nuts.

Nutritional Information per Serving:

Calories 138| Fat 4g |Sodium 36mg | Carbs 25.2g | Fiber 0.5g | Sugar 16g | Protein 1.2g

Peanut Butter Fudge

Prep Time: 10 minutes

Cook Time: 5 minutes

Serves: 2

Ingredients

- ⅓ cup icing sugar

- 1 tablespoon peanut butter

- 4 tablespoons cocoa powder

- 2 teaspoons milk

- ⅓ teaspoon soft butter

- ¼ teaspoon vanilla

Directions

1. Combine all the ingredients in a bowl. Mix well.

2. Spread the prepared mixture in the prepared baking pan.

3. Bake in the oven for 5 minutes.

4. Allow the fudge to cool completely before serving.

Serving Suggestion: Serve with chocolate milk.

Variation Tip: You can use margarine instead of butter.

Nutritional Information per Serving:

Calories 159 | Fat 6.2g | Sodium 46mg | Carbs 28g | Fiber 3.7g | Sugar 20.1g | Protein 4.1g

Rice Krispies Treats

Prep Time: 40 minutes

Cook Time: 5 minutes

Serves: 2

Ingredients

- 2 teaspoons butter
- 4 teaspoons marshmallow cream
- 4 tablespoons Rice Krispies cereal

Directions

1. Combine the marshmallow cream and butter in a bowl. Place them in the prepared baking pan.

2. Melt them in the oven for 5 minutes.

3. Mix the cereal with the marshmallow mixture.

4. Form the mixture into cookie shapes. Place the shapes on a plate and put them in the refrigerator until they become solid (about 30 minutes).

5. Serve!

Serving Suggestion: Serve with a drizzle of chocolate syrup on top.

Variation Tip: Use margarine instead of butter.

Nutritional Information per Serving:

Calories 214 | Fat 6g | Sodium 88mg | Carbs 38g | Fiber 0g | Sugar 20g | Protein 1g

Popcorn Balls

Prep Time: 10 minutes

Cook Time: 2 minutes

Serves: 1

Ingredients

- ½ cup caramel syrup, candy, or topping
- ½ cup popped popcorn, unsalted

Directions

1. Put the caramel in the prepared baking pan and melt it in the oven for 2 minutes.

2. Pour the caramel over the popcorn.

3. Using your hands, form small balls from the mixture. Place on a parchment paper-lined plate.

4. Chill the popcorn balls before serving.

Serving Suggestion: Serve with salted nuts.

Variation Tip: None, this recipe is delicious as it is!

Nutritional Information per Serving:

Calories 116 | Fat 0.1g | Sodium 18mg | Carbs 27.7g | Fiber 0.3g | Sugar 25g | Protein 0.3g

Chocolate Covered Pretzels

Prep Time: 10 minutes

Cook Time: 5 minutes

Serves: 3

Ingredients

- ½ cup mini chocolate chips
- 1 teaspoon shortening
- 10 pretzel rods
- ¼ cup colored sugar, for decoration

Directions

1. Put the shortening and chocolate chips in the prepared baking pan and melt them in the oven for 5 minutes.

2. Once melted, spoon the mixture over the pretzels.

3. Sprinkle the colored sugar on top of the pretzels.

4. Once all the pretzels are coated, place them in the refrigerator to set.

5. Serve and enjoy.

Serving Suggestion: Serve with flavored milk.

Variation Tip: Use caramel syrup instead of colored sugar.

Nutritional Information per Serving:

Calories 400 | Fat 3g | Sodium 1995mg | Carbs 87g | Fiber 2.6g | Sugar 7.6g | Protein 7g

Bacon Roll-Ups

Prep Time: 10 minutes

Cook Time: 15 minutes

Serves: 1

Ingredients

- ⅛ cup sour cream
- ¼ tablespoon onion salt
- 1 tablespoon bacon bits
- 1 can crescent roll

Directions

1. Combine the sour cream, onion salt, and bacon bits in a bowl.

2. Separate out the crescent roll and spread the mixture over it.

3. Cut into pieces and roll each piece up.

4. Put the rolls on the prepared baking pan.

5. Bake in the oven for 15 minutes.

Serving Suggestion: Serve with cheese sauce.

Variation Tip: Use plain salt instead of onion salt.

Nutritional Information per Serving:

Calories 356 | Fat 13g | Sodium 414mg | Carbs 36g | Fiber 4g | Sugar 1g | Protein 19g

Cheese Balls

Prep Time: 12 minutes

Cook Time: 15 minutes

Serves: 2

Ingredients

- 2 tablespoons margarine
- 1 tablespoon self-rising flour
- $\frac{1}{3}$ cup cheese, grated
- ¼ cup Rice Krispies

Directions

1. Mix all the ingredients in a bowl. Combine well.
2. Shape small balls from the mixture with your hands.
3. Place the balls on the prepared baking pan.
4. Bake for 15 minutes.

Serving Suggestion: Serve with your choice of dip.

Variation Tip: Use your favorite type of cheese.

Nutritional Information per Serving:

Calories 840 | Fat 14g | Sodium 1843mg | Carbs 93.1g | Fiber 0.4g | Sugar 44g | Protein 25g

Cinnamon Bread Pudding

Prep Time: 10 minutes

Cook Time: 25 minutes

Serves: 2

Ingredients

- 1 egg
- ½ cup milk
- ¼ teaspoon vanilla extract
- 4 tablespoons sugar
- 4 slices white bread

Topping

- Pinch of cinnamon
- 1 teaspoon milk
- ½ teaspoon butter, melted

Directions

1. Break the bread into pieces.

2. Mix the bread pieces with the milk, vanilla, and sugar in a bowl.

3. Fill two prepared baking pans halfway up with the mixture, and then press down. (It doesn't matter if you don't have two pans. You will need to cook in two batches anyway.)

4. Pour the milk and butter on top. Sprinkle with the cinnamon.

5. Bake one pan at a time for 25 minutes each.

Serving Suggestion: Serve with ice cream.

Variation Tip: Use brown bread instead of white bread.

Nutritional Information per Serving:

Calories 212 | Fat 5.3g | Sodium 190mg | Carbs 36.4g | Fiber 0.4g | Sugar 27.8g | Protein 6.2g

Cheesy Biscuits

Prep Time: 15 minutes

Cook Time: 12 minutes

Serves: 2

Ingredients

- $1/3$ cup butter, softened
- 2 cups cheddar cheese, grated
- 1 cup all-purpose flour
- Pinch of salt
- Pinch of cayenne pepper

Directions

1. Mix the butter, cheese, salt, and cayenne pepper in a large bowl. Combine well.

2. Add the flour and mix well.

3. Roll out the dough on a floured surface.

4. Cut the dough into small rounds and then roll into balls.

5. Place on the prepared baking pan.

6. Bake in the oven for 12 minutes.

Serving Suggestion: Serve with a sauce of your choice.

Variation Tip: You can use any cheese you like.

Nutritional Information per Serving:

Calories 954 | Fat 68.8g | Sodium 998mg | Carbs 50g | Fiber 1.7g | Sugar 0.8g | Protein 34.9g

Almond Cookies

Prep Time: 10 minutes

Cook Time: 20 minutes

Serves: 2

Ingredients

- 3 tablespoons butter
- 1½ tablespoons icing sugar
- ⅛ teaspoon of vanilla
- ¼ cup almond flour
- Pinch of salt
- 2 tablespoons almonds, chopped

Directions

1. Mix the butter, icing sugar, vanilla, almond flour, and salt in a bowl.

2. Blend well, and then add the chopped almonds. Combine well.

3. Shape the mixture into balls and place them on the prepared baking pan.

4. Flatten the balls slightly with your hand.

5. Bake for 5 minutes.

6. Once cool, serve. Enjoy!

Serving Suggestion: Serve with shredded coconut sprinkled on top and a drizzle of melted chocolate.

Variation Tip: Use shortening instead of butter.

Nutritional Information per Serving:

Calories 291| Fat 24g | Sodium 78mg | Carbs 16.5g | Fiber 1g | Sugar 3.8g | Protein 3.5g

Snowball Cookies

Prep Time: 10 minutes

Cook Time: 9 minutes

Serves: 2

Ingredients

- 6 teaspoons butter, softened
- 3 teaspoons powdered sugar, plus extra for rolling
- $\frac{1}{8}$ teaspoon vanilla extract
- ¼ cup flour
- Dash of sea salt
- 4 teaspoons walnuts, chopped

Directions

1. Combine all the ingredients in a bowl.
2. Carefully shape the mixture into 1-inch balls and roll them in some powdered sugar.
3. Place the balls in the prepared baking pan and then slightly press down on each of them with your hand.
4. Bake in the oven for 9 minutes.
5. Once done, roll in some more sugar.

Serving Suggestion: Serve with flavored milk.

Variation Tip: None, these cookies are yummy as they are!

Nutritional Information per Serving:

Calories 267 | Fat 16.2g | Sodium 159mg | Carbs 27.7g | Fiber 1g | Sugar 14.7g | Protein 3.6g

Sugar Cookies

Prep Time: 10 minutes

Cook Time: 10 minutes

Serves: 2

Ingredients

- 8 teaspoons butter
- 4 teaspoons sugar
- 2 teaspoons brown sugar
- Salt
- ¼ cup flour
- $1/3$ teaspoon baking powder
- $1/3$ teaspoon vanilla extract

Directions

1. Mix the butter, salt, and sugar in a bowl.
2. Add the baking powder, flour, and vanilla.
3. Mix well.
4. Form cookie-shaped pieces from the batter and place them on the prepared baking pan.
5. Bake for 10 minutes.
6. Cool and enjoy!

Serving Suggestion: Serve the cookies with milk.

Variation Tip: None, the cookies are simple but delicious!

Nutritional Information per Serving:

Calories 238 | Fat 15.7g | Sodium 188mg | Carbs 23.4g | Fiber 0.4g | Sugar 11.1g | Protein 1.8g

Oatmeal Cookies

Prep Time: 10 minutes (plus 3 hours for refrigeration)

Cook Time: 20–40 minutes

Serves: 2

Ingredients

- ¼ cup shortening
- ¼ cup butter
- ½ cup icing sugar, stifled
- ½ teaspoon vanilla extract
- ¾ cup all-purpose flour
- $1/3$ cup rolled oats, uncooked

Directions

1. Mix together the shortening, butter, and icing sugar in a bowl.

2. Add in the remaining ingredients.

3. On a floured surface, shape the dough into a 7-inch-long log.

4. Wrap the dough in plastic wrap. Refrigerate the dough for 3 hours.

5. Take the dough out from the refrigerator. Remove the wrap. Slice it into ¼-inch rounds.

6. Place half of the rounds in the prepared baking pan (or as many that will fit).

7. Bake for 20–40 minutes.

8. Repeat for the next batch(es).

Serving Suggestion: Serve with flavored milk.

Variation Tip: Use margarine instead of butter.

Nutritional Information per Serving:

Calories 749 | Fat 49.6g | Sodium 165mg | Carbs 70.4g | Fiber 1.9g | Sugar 0.4g | Protein 6g

Pecan Cookies

Prep Time: 10 minutes (plus 3 hours for refrigeration)

Cook Time: 20 minutes

Serves: 2

Ingredients

- $1/3$ cup all-purpose flour
- ¼ teaspoon of cinnamon
- Pinch of salt
- 10 tablespoons unsalted butter, softened
- $1/3$ cup sugar
- 1 teaspoon vanilla extract
- 4 pecans, toasted and chopped

Directions

1. Mix the butter, vanilla, and sugar in a bowl.

2. Blend well until the mixture becomes creamy in texture.

3. Add the cinnamon, salt, flour, and pecans. Blend well to make a soft dough.

4. Place the dough on a floured surface and form it into a log shape.

5. Wrap the log in plastic wrap and refrigerate for 3 hours.

6. Take the dough out of the refrigerator. Remove the wrap.

7. Cut the dough into cookie rounds. Place the rounds onto the prepared baking pan. (You will probably need to cook several batches.)

8. Bake for 20 minutes. Cool on a cooling rack.

Serving Suggestion: Serve with a sprinkle of powdered sugar.

Variation Tip: None, these cookies are delicious!

Nutritional Information per Serving:

Calories 912 | Fat 77.8g | Sodium 487mg | Carbs 53.8g | Fiber 3.7g | Sugar 34.7g | Protein 5.8g

Potato Drop Cookies

Prep Time: 10 minutes

Cook Time: 10 minutes

Serves: 2

Ingredients

- 2 tablespoons shortening
- 2 tablespoons sugar
- 2 tablespoons brown sugar
- 1 egg
- $\frac{1}{8}$ teaspoon vanilla extract
- $\frac{1}{4}$ cup all-purpose flour
- $\frac{1}{8}$ teaspoon baking soda
- $\frac{1}{8}$ teaspoon salt
- $\frac{1}{4}$ cup potato chips, crushed

Directions

1. Mix the shortening and sugars in a bowl until fluffy and creamy.

2. Add in the vanilla and the remaining ingredients. Combine well.

3. Drop spoonfuls of the mixture onto the prepared baking pan.

4. Bake for 8–10 minutes.

5. Let the cookies cool completely before serving.

Serving Suggestion: Serve with milk.

Variation Tip: Use white sugar instead of brown sugar.

Nutritional Information per Serving:

Calories 416 | Fat 24.4g | Sodium 389mg | Carbs 47g | Fiber 1.7g | Sugar 21g | Protein 4.2g

Rosemary Biscuits

Prep Time: 10 minutes

Cook Time: 15 minutes

Serves: 2

Ingredients

- 1 can Pillsbury Biscuits
- 1 sprig rosemary, finely chopped
- ½ teaspoon salt

Directions

1. Lay the biscuits on the prepared baking pan and sprinkle with the rosemary and salt.

2. Bake the biscuits for 13–16 minutes or until their edges are golden.

Serving Suggestion: Serve with cheese.

Variation Tip: You can use dried herbs.

Nutritional Information per Serving:

Calories 97 | Fat 4.2g | Sodium 897mg | Carbs 12.4g | Fiber 0.4g | Sugar 2.1g | Protein 2.1g

Chocolate and Oatmeal Cookies

Prep Time: 10 minutes

Cook Time: 12 minutes

Serves: 3

Ingredients

- 1 sachet low-sugar instant oatmeal
- 4 tablespoons flour
- 2 tablespoons butter, room temperature
- ⅛ tablespoon baking soda
- ⅛ teaspoon baking powder
- 3 tablespoons mini chocolate chips
- ⅛ teaspoon vanilla extract
- 1 tablespoon brown sugar
- 1 tablespoon white sugar
- 4 tablespoons water

Directions

1. Mix all the ingredients in a bowl using a hand mixer. Combine thoroughly.

2. Place teaspoon-sized drops of the mixture onto the prepared baking pan. (You will need to cook the cookies in batches.)

3. Bake for 12 minutes and then allow to cool on a cooling rack.

Serving Suggestion: Serve the cookies with milk.

Variation Tip: You can use dark, milk, or white chocolate chips.

Nutritional Information per Serving:

Calories 258 | Fat 12.7g | Sodium 229mg | Carbs 34.4g | Fiber 1.9g | Sugar 12.4g | Protein 3.7g

Snow Mound Cookies

Prep Time: 10 minutes

Cook Time: 5 minutes

Serves: 2

Ingredients

- 6 teaspoons shortening
- 3 teaspoons icing sugar, plus extra for rolling
- $\frac{1}{8}$ teaspoon vanilla extract
- ¼ cup flour
- Pinch of salt
- 2 tablespoons walnuts, finely chopped

Directions

1. Mix all the ingredients in a bowl. Combine well.

2. Make small ball shapes from the mixture

(about 1 inch in size).

3. Place three balls at a time on the prepared baking pan.

4. Flatten them slightly with your hand.

5. Bake for 5 minutes.

6. Bake the next batch.

7. Let the cookies cool completely before rolling in more icing sugar.

Serving Suggestion: Serve the cookies with milk.

Variation Tip: You can use soft butter instead of shortening.

Nutritional Information per Serving:

Calories 234 | Fat 17.2g | Sodium 78mg | Carbs 16.5g | Fiber 1g | Sugar 3.8g | Protein 3.5g

Princess Cookies

Prep Time: 10 minutes (plus 45 minutes for refrigeration)

Cook Time: 10 minutes

Serves: 4

Ingredients

- 2 cups all-purpose flour
- 1 teaspoon baking powder or baking soda
- Pinch of salt
- 1 cup unsalted butter, softened
- 1 cup white sugar
- 2 small eggs
- ⅓ cup lemon juice
- ½ teaspoon lemon zest
- ¼ teaspoon vanilla extract

Directions

1. Mix the flour, baking soda, salt, zest, and sugar in a bowl.

2. In a separate bowl, beat the butter with the sugar using an electric hand beater. Then add the eggs. Combine well.

3. Add the vanilla extract and lemon juice. Mix well.

4. Add the flour mixture to the egg mixture. Mix well.

5. Chill the dough for about 45 minutes.

6. Form cookie shapes from the dough and place them onto the prepared baking pan. You'll have to cook in batches.

7. Bake for 10 minutes.

8. Once done, take out and cool on a wire rack.

Serving Suggestion: Serve with milk.

Variation Tip: Use brown sugar instead of white sugar.

Nutritional Information per Serving:

Calories 674 | Fat 48.9g | Sodium 399mg | Carbs 50g | Fiber 1.8g | Sugar 2.2g | Protein 9.7g

Chocolate Chip Cookies

Prep Time: 10 minutes

Cook Time: 24 minutes

Serves: 2

Ingredients

- 2 teaspoons brown sugar
- 2 teaspoons white sugar
- 1 stick margarine
- $\frac{1}{8}$ teaspoon baking soda or baking powder
- $\frac{1}{8}$ teaspoon vanilla extract
- 2 teaspoons water
- 4 tablespoons all-purpose flour
- 3–4 teaspoons mini chocolate chips

Directions

1. Whisk the brown and white sugar with the margarine in a bowl using a hand beater

2. Add the vanilla, baking powder, sugar water, and flour

3. Blend until all the ingredients are well combined.

4. Add the chocolate chips, and mix well.

5. Roll the mixture between your fingers to make small balls of about ½ an inch.

6. Place the balls on the prepared baking pan. You will need to cook in batches.

7. Bake for 12 minutes.

Serving Suggestion: Serve with milk.

Variation Tip: Use butter instead of margarine.

Nutritional Information per Serving:

Calories 317 | Fat 12g | Sodium 166mg | Carbs 48g | Fiber 0.3g | Sugar 26.4g | Protein 3.3g

Angel Food Cake Mix Cookies

Prep Time: 10 minutes

Cook Time: 20 minutes

Serves: 3

Ingredients

- 1 box angel food cake mix
- ½ cup pineapple soda

Directions

1. Using a hand mixer, blend the soda with the angel food cake mix in a bowl.

2. Place heaped tablespoons of the mixture onto the baking pan. Don't put the cookies too close together. You'll need to cook in batches.

3. Bake for 20 minutes or until the tops become light golden brown.

4. Remove and allow them to cool on a wire rack.

Serving Suggestion: Serve with your favorite toppings.

Variation Tip: Use any other flavor of soda you prefer.

Nutritional Information per Serving:

Calories 72 | Fat 0.2g | Sodium 65mg | Carbs 16.7g| Fiber 0g | Sugar 13.7g | Protein 1g

Banana Cream Cake

Prep Time: 10 minutes

Cook Time: 15 minutes

Serves: 2

Ingredients

- 8 tablespoons flour
- 5 teaspoons sugar
- ½ teaspoon baking powder
- Dash of salt
- 8 teaspoons milk
- 3 teaspoons shortening
- 4 tablespoons banana cream pudding mix

Directions

1. Combine the sugar, salt, and baking powder in a bowl, and then add the shortening.

2. Stir until the batter becomes smooth.

3. Add the pudding mix and mix well.

4. Pour in the milk and mix well.

5. Pour the batter into the prepared baking pan.

6. Bake for 15 minutes.

7. Remove the cake and let it cool before serving.

Serving Suggestion: Serve with a whipped cream topping.

Variation Tip: None, this cake is delicious as it is!

Nutritional Information per Serving:

Calories 399 | Fat 7.1g | Sodium 729mg | Carbs 81g | Fiber 0.9g | Sugar 49g | Protein 3.9g

Cornbread

Prep Time: 15 minutes

Cook Time: 15 minutes

Serves: 2

Ingredients

- 1 tablespoon white sugar
- Pinch of salt
- 2 teaspoons butter, softened
- ¼ teaspoon vanilla extract
- ¼ cup all-purpose flour
- ½ teaspoon baking powder
- 1 tablespoon cornmeal
- 2 tablespoons milk

Directions

1. Beat the butter, sugar, and salt in a bowl.
2. Add the milk and vanilla extract.
3. Take a separate bowl and combine the baking powder, flour, and cornmeal.
4. Stir the flour mixture into the sugar mixture. Combine well.
5. Put the batter into the prepared baking pan.
6. Bake for 15 minutes.
7. Once it's done, let it cool and serve.

Serving Suggestion: Serve with milk.

Variation Tip: Use almond milk instead of dairy.

Nutritional Information per Serving:

Calories 137 | Fat 4.4g | Sodium 115mg | Carbs 22.3g | Fiber 0.7g | Sugar 6.8g | Protein 2.5g

Pretty Pink Cake

Prep Time: 10 minutes

Cook Time: 12 minutes

Serves: 3

Ingredients

- 5 tablespoons cake flour
- ¼ teaspoon baking powder
- $\frac{1}{8}$ teaspoon salt
- 5 teaspoons red sugar crystals
- ¼ teaspoon vanilla extract
- 4 teaspoons vegetable oil
- 8 teaspoons milk

Directions

1. Combine the cake mix, baking powder, salt, and sugar in a bowl

2. Gently pour in the milk and mix well.

3. Add the remaining ingredients and mix until a smooth pink batter is formed.

4. Pour the batter into the prepared baking pan.

5. Bake for 15 minutes.

6. Allow the cake to cool completely before serving.

Serving Suggestion: Serve with colored frosting and decorations of your choice.

Variation Tip: None, this cake is delicious as it is!

Nutritional Information per Serving:

Calories 134 | Fat 6.5g | Sodium 104mg | Carbs 16g | Fiber 0.4g | Sugar 5.7g | Protein 1.8g

Lemon Cake

Prep Time: 10 minutes

Cook Time: 12–15minutes

Serves: 3

Ingredients

- 1 cup sugar
- 1½ cups flour
- 1 teaspoon baking soda
- ½ teaspoon salt
- 1 teaspoon lemon-flavored drink mix
- ⅓ cup shortening

Directions

1. Take a bowl and mix the flour, baking soda, sugar, salt, and lemonade drink mix. Combine well.

2. Add in the shortening with a fork until well combined.

3. Use ⅓ cup of the mixture at a time. You can store the rest in Ziploc bags for up to 12 weeks.

4. Mix ⅓ cup of the mixture with 4 teaspoons of water in a bowl.

5. Put the mixture into the prepared baking pan.

6. Bake for 12–15 minutes. Allow the cake to cool before serving.

Serving Suggestion: Serve with cream.

Variation Tip: Use baking powder instead of baking soda.

Nutritional Information per Serving:

Calories 499 | Fat 22.8g | Sodium 813mg | Carbs 77g | Fiber 0.2g | Sugar 69g | Protein 1g

Tea Cake

Prep Time: 10 minutes

Cook Time: 15 minutes

Serves: 2

Ingredients

- 1 cup all-purpose flour
- 1 teaspoon baking powder
- ½ teaspoon salt
- 4 teaspoons sugar
- 3 teaspoons margarine
- ¾ cup milk

Directions

1. Mix the flour, baking powder, salt, margarine, and sugar to a lightly crumbly consistency.

2. Pour in the milk slowly and combine to make a creamy consistency.

3. Pour half of the mixture into the prepared pan. (Cook the other half next.) Bake for 15 minutes.

Serving Suggestion: Serve with tea.

Variation Tip: Use almond milk instead of dairy.

Nutritional Information per Serving:

Calories 130 | Fat 4.9g | Sodium 219mg | Carbs 19.4g | Fiber 0.5g | Sugar 5.6g | Protein 2.2g

Peanut Butter Cake

Prep Time: 10 minutes

Cook Time: 30 minutes

Serves: 2

Ingredients

- 1 tablespoon peanut butter
- 2 tablespoons milk
- 4 tablespoons yellow cake mix

Directions

1. Mix the yellow cake mix, peanut butter, and milk in a bowl and stir well.

2. Pour half of the mixture into the prepared pan. You will bake the other half next.

3. Bake for 15 minutes. Repeat with the other half of the mixture.

4. Once done, allow to cool completely.

Serving Suggestion: Serve with flavored milk.

Variation Tip: None, this cake is yummy as it is!

Nutritional Information per Serving:

Calories 224 | Fat 10.2g |Sodium 259mg | Carbs 28.5g | Fiber 1.3g | Sugar 2.9g | Protein 6.3g

Toffee Trifle Cake

Prep Time: 10 minutes

Cook Time: 15minutes

Serves: 2–3

Ingredients

- 8 tablespoons yellow cake mix
- 3 tablespoons milk
- 1 small box instant pudding mix, vanilla flavor
- 1$\frac{1}{3}$ cups cold milk
- 1 cup Cool Whip
- 2 candy bars, crushed

Directions

1. Combine the yellow cake mix and milk in a bowl. Mix until smooth.

2. Pour the mixture into the prepared baking pan and bake for 15 minutes.

3. Let the cake cool completely, and then cut it into small cubes.

4. Whisk together the cold milk and pudding mix.

5. Fold in the Cool Whip.

6. Take two or three glass bowls, and start arranging the pieces of cake in the bottom of each.

7. Cover with a generous amount of pudding mixture, and then sprinkle on some of the crushed candy.

8. Repeat the layers until all the ingredients are used.

9. Refrigerate for 2 hours before serving.

Serving Suggestion: Top with some more Cool Whip and chocolate shavings.

Variation Tip: Use any kind of candy bar you like.

Nutritional Information per Serving:

Calories 220 | Fat 12.1g | Sodium 142mg | Carbs 25.6g | Fiber 0.6g | Sugar 18.3g | Protein 2.9g

Red Velvet Cake

Prep Time: 15 minutes

Cook Time: 15 minutes

Serves: 2

Ingredients

- 3 tablespoons flour
- $\frac{1}{6}$ teaspoon baking soda
- Dash of salt
- 1½ tablespoons red sugar crystals
- $\frac{1}{6}$ teaspoon vanilla
- 3 teaspoons vegetable oil
- 6 teaspoons milk
- Pink frosting or buttercream, for decoration

Directions

1. Mix the cake flour, red sugar crystals, vanilla, oil, milk, salt, and baking soda in a bowl.

2. Mix it into a smooth batter.

3. Pour the batter into the prepared baking pan.

4. Bake for 15 minutes

5. Frost it with the frosting or buttercream.

Serving Suggestion: Serve the cake with ice cream.

Variation Tip: You can use red food coloring instead of red sugar crystals.

Nutritional Information per Serving:

Calories 146 | Fat 7.2g | Sodium 95mg | Carbs 17.3g | Fiber 0.3g | Sugar 8.1g | Protein 1.7g

Vanilla Cake

Prep Time: 10 minutes

Cook Time: 12–14 minutes

Serves: 2

Ingredients

- ½ cup margarine
- ¾ cup white sugar
- ¾ cup brown sugar
- 1 teaspoon vanilla
- 1 egg
- 1½ cups vanilla cake mix
- ¼ teaspoon baking soda
- Pinch of salt

Directions

1. Whisk the egg in a bowl and then add the white sugar, brown sugar, vanilla, baking soda, salt, and margarine.

2. Mix together well.

3. Add the all-purpose flour and mix well.

4. Pour the mixture into the prepared baking pan. You may need to cook in batches.

5. Bake for 12–14 minutes.

6. Allow the cake to cool before serving.

Serving Suggestion: Top with vanilla buttercream and colored sprinkles.

Variation Tip: Use butter instead of margarine.

Nutritional Information per Serving:

Calories 425 | Fat 10.5g | Sodium 1250mg | Carbs 83.1g | Fiber 0.5g | Sugar 75 g | Protein 1.5g

Chocolate Birthday Cake

Prep Time: 10 minutes

Cook Time: 20 minutes

Serves: 1

Ingredients (x2 to make 2 layers)

- 2 tablespoons all-purpose flour
- 1 tablespoon dark cocoa
- 1 tablespoon white or brown sugar
- $\frac{1}{8}$ teaspoon baking soda
- Dash of salt
- $\frac{1}{8}$ teaspoon vanilla extract
- 4 teaspoons water
- 1 tablespoon olive oil or vegetable oil

Directions

1. Mix the sugar, oil, cocoa, flour, baking soda, salt, water, and vanilla extract in a bowl. Combine well.

2. Pour the prepared batter into the prepared baking pan.

3. Bake for 20 minutes.

4. Repeat the whole process to make another layer.

5. Let the cakes cool completely before serving.

Serving Suggestion: Put buttercream or frosting of your choice on the top of one cake and place the other cake on top. Then put buttercream or frosting on top. Serve with vanilla ice cream.

Variation Tip: Use chocolate syrup instead of cocoa powder.

Nutritional Information per Serving:

Calories 172 | Fat 9.6g | Sodium 157mg | Carbs 22.2g | Fiber 1.4g | Sugar 12g | Protein 1.7g

Chocolate Lava Cake

Prep Time: 10 minutes

Cook Time: 15 minutes

Serves: 2

Ingredients

- ⅓ cup butter
- ⅓ cup semi-sweet chocolate chips
- ¾ cup powdered sugar
- 2 eggs
- 6 tablespoons cornstarch

Directions

1. Place two greased ramekins on the oven's baking pan.

2. Put the chocolate chips and butter in a microwave-safe bowl and heat in the microwave until melted.

3. Add the sugar and stir well.

4. Add in the eggs and combine until smooth.

5. Add the cornstarch and stir well.

6. Divide the batter between the ramekins.

7. Bake for 15 minutes.

Serving Suggestion: Serve with vanilla ice cream.

Variation Tip: None, this recipe is delicious!

Nutritional Information per Serving:

Calories 776 | Fat 45.1g | Sodium 282mg | Carbs 89.9g | Fiber 2.7g | Sugar 54.4g | Protein 8.4g

Easy Baked Alaska

Prep Time: 10 minutes (plus 4 hours for freezing)

Cook Time: 20 minutes

Serves: 3

Ingredients

- 3 cups Neapolitan ice cream, slightly softened
- ½-pound cake, sliced into 1-inch-thick pieces
- 3 egg whites
- ½ teaspoon cream of tartar
- ¾ cup sugar

Directions

1. Take a bowl and line it with plastic wrap.

2. Scoop the ice cream into the bowl. Press it in to make sure no spaces are showing.

3. Top the ice cream with the pound cake slices, cutting them if necessary to ensure the ice cream is completely covered.

4. Gently press the cake into the ice cream.

5. Cover and freeze for 3 hours.

6. When the cake is frozen, beat together the egg whites and cream of tartar.

7. Once smooth, add the sugar and beat until stiff peaks form.

8. Invert the frozen cake onto the baking pan. Remove the plastic wrap.

9. Cover the cake with the meringue and freeze for at least 1 hour.

10. Bake the cake for 5 minutes, or until the meringue is golden.

Serving Suggestion: Serve sliced with whipped cream.

Variation Tip: None, this recipe is yummy!

Nutritional Information per Serving:

Calories 618 | Fat 18g | Sodium 349mg | Carbs 111g | Fiber 0.2g | Sugar 62g | Protein 8.3g

Pretty Rose Cake

Prep Time: 10 minutes

Cook Time: 25 minutes

Serves: 3

Ingredients

- 1½ cups all-purpose flour
- ¾ cup powdered sugar
- 2 teaspoons baking powder
- ½ cup milk
- ¼ cup cooking oil
- ¼ cup + 1 tablespoon of Rose syrup
- $^{1}/_{3}$ teaspoon rose essence

Directions

1. Mix all the dry ingredients in a bowl.

2. In a separate bowl, mix all the liquid ingredients.

3. Combine the ingredients of both bowls together.

4. Pour the batter into the prepared baking pan.

5. Bake for 25 minutes or until a toothpick inserted into the center of the cake comes out clean.

6. Allow the cake to cool before serving.

Serving Suggestion: Serve with milk.

Variation Tip: None, this cake is delicious as it is!

Nutritional Information per Serving:

Calories 601 | Fat 19.6g | Sodium 23mg | Carbs 101g | Fiber 1.8g | Sugar 52.1g | Protein 7.8g

Party Cake

Prep Time: 10 minutes

Cook Time: 10 minutes

Serves: 2

Ingredients

- ½ cup all-purpose flour
- ½ teaspoon baking powder
- ¼ teaspoon salt
- 4 teaspoons sugar
- 4 teaspoons margarine
- 8 teaspoons milk
- Multi-colored cookie decorations.

Directions

1. Take a bowl and add the flour, baking powder, sugar, margarine, and salt.

2. Combine well, and then add in the milk.

3. Once the batter is ready, pour it into the prepared baking pan.

4. Sprinkle the top of the batter with the cookie decorations.

5. Bake for about 10 minutes or until a toothpick inserted into the center of the cake comes out clean.

Serving Suggestion: Allow the cake to cool completely, and then add frosting or buttercream of your choice.

Variation Tip: Use butter instead of margarine.

Nutritional Information per Serving:

Calories 443 | Fat 16.3g | Sodium 479mg | Carbs 67.5g | Fiber 0.9g | Sugar 25g | Protein 6g

Little Prince Bars (With Dulce de Leche)

Prep Time: 10 minutes (plus 2 hours for chilling)

Cook Time: 12 minutes

Serves: 2

Ingredients

- ½ cup unsalted butter
- 4 tablespoons water
- Pinch of salt
- ½ cup white sugar
- 1 teaspoon baking powder
- 1 cup plain all-purpose flour
- Dulce de leche, for serving

Directions

1. Put the butter, salt, water, and sugar in a saucepan over low heat.

2. Bring the mixture to a boil.

3. Remove the saucepan from the heat. Mix well.

4. Once the mixture is cool, add the flour and baking powder. Mix well.

5. Form the mixture into a ball. Place it in the refrigerator for 2 hours.

6. Roll the dough out between sheets of parchment paper.

7. Cut the dough into equal-sized squares.

8. Place the squares onto the prepared baking pan. You'll need to cook in batches.

9. Bake for about 12 minutes.

10. Let them cool completely on a wire rack before serving.

Serving Suggestion: Apply a good amount of dulce de leche to the top of one square. Place another square on top. Repeat until all the squares are used up.

Variation Tip: You can use another type of filling if you prefer.

Nutritional Information per Serving:

Calories 1041| Fat 46.6g | Sodium 420mg | Carbs 153g | Fiber 1.9g | Sugar 50.g | Protein 2.2g

Baby Brownies

Prep Time: 10 minutes

Cook Time: 30 minutes

Serves: 3

Ingredients

- 8 ounces semi-sweet chocolate
- $1/3$ cup chocolate syrup
- 10 tablespoons unsalted butter, at room temperature
- 1 teaspoon vanilla extract
- 2 eggs, lightly beaten
- ¼ cup sugar
- Pinch of salt
- ½ cup all-purpose flour

Directions

1. Melt the chocolate in a saucepan over low heat, stirring constantly.

2. Add the syrup and stir until combined.

3. Remove the pan from the heat and add the butter.

4. Beat the mixture until smooth.

5. Add the vanilla and eggs. Mix well.

6. In another mixing bowl, add the flour, sugar, and salt. Mix well to combine.

7. Add the flour mixture to the chocolate mixture. Combine well.

8. Pour the batter into the prepared baking pan.

9. Bake for 30 minutes.

10. Allow the brownies to cool completely before cutting them into 1-inch squares and serving.

Serving Suggestion: Serve the brownies drizzled with chocolate syrup.

Variation Tip: None; the brownies are yummy as they are.

Nutritional Information per Serving:

Calories 979 | Fat 64g | Sodium 397mg | Carbs 102g | Fiber 6g | Sugar 75g | Protein 10.1g

Six Layer Bars

Prep Time: 10 minutes

Cook Time: 20 minutes

Serves: 3

Ingredients

- 2 tablespoons margarine
-  ⅓ cup graham cracker crumbs
- 2 tablespoons semi-sweet chocolate chips
- 3 tablespoons butterscotch chips
- 4 tablespoons coconut flakes
- 2 tablespoons condensed milk
- 1 tablespoon chopped walnuts

Directions

1. Melt the margarine in the microwave. Place it into the baking pan.

2. Spread the graham cracker crumbs evenly over the melted margarine.

3. Add a layer of chocolate chips and then a layer of butterscotch chips.

4. Add a layer of flaked coconut and walnuts.

5. Pour the condensed milk over the top.

6. Bake for 15–20 minutes.

7. Allow the bar to cool completely before cutting into pieces and serving.

Serving Suggestion: Serve with milk.

Variation Tip: Any other nuts can be used instead of walnuts.

Nutritional Information per Serving:

Calories 317 | Fat 20.8g | Sodium 226mg | Carbs 3.6g | Fiber 2.4g | Sugar 21.7g | Protein 3.2g

Apple Bar

Prep Time: 15 minutes

Cook Time: 20 minutes

Serves: 2

Ingredients

- 3 tablespoons all-purpose flour
- 1 tablespoon crushed cornflakes
- 1 tablespoon soft butter
- $\frac{1}{8}$ teaspoon ground cinnamon
- 1 teaspoon sugar
- 2 teaspoons apple jelly

Directions

1. Take a large bowl and combine the flour, cereal, butter, cinnamon, and sugar in it.

2. Mix until the mixture becomes crumbly. Set aside 2–3 tablespoons to use later.

3. Press the rest of the mixture into the prepared baking pan.

4. Spread the apple jelly over the top of the mixture.

5. Sprinkle the reserved crumbly mixture over the jelly.

6. Slightly press the mixture in with your fingers.

7. Bake for 20 minutes.

8. Once done, let it cool and then cut it into wedges.

9. Enjoy!

Serving Suggestion: Serve with whipped cream.

Variation Tip: None, this recipe is delicious!

Nutritional Information per Serving:

Calories 136 | Fat 2.9g | Sodium 58mg | Carbs 25.6g | Fiber 1.1g | Sugar 5.5g | Protein 2.8g

Orange Marmalade Bars

Prep Time: 10 minutes

Cook Time: 21 minutes

Serves: 2

Ingredients

- 1 tablespoon butter, softened
- 4 teaspoons sugar
- $\frac{1}{3}$ cup flour
- 4 tablespoons almond milk
- $\frac{1}{6}$ teaspoon baking soda
- 2 tablespoons quick-cook rolled oats
- Dash of salt
- 5 teaspoons orange marmalade

Directions

1. Mix the sugar and butter along with the salt in a bowl until creamy.

2. Add the baking soda, flour, milk, and oats. Mix well.

3. Divide the batter into two prepared baking pans.

4. Press down a little on the mixture.

5. Spread the orange marmalade on the top of each.

6. Bake each for 21 minutes.

7. Once done, let the bars cool completely and then cut into small slices.

8. Serve and enjoy!

Serving Suggestion: Serve as a snack.

Variation Tip: Use coconut milk instead of almond milk

Nutritional Information per Serving:

Calories 269 | Fat 13.3g | Sodium 236mg | Carbs 36.6g | Fiber 1.6g | Sugar 16.9g | Protein 3.9g

Easy-Bake Oven Brownies

Prep Time: 10 minutes

Cook Time: 15 minutes

Serves: 2

Ingredients

- 2 tablespoons sugar
- 2 tablespoons flour
- ½ teaspoon margarine
- ⅙ teaspoon vanilla extract
- 5 teaspoons chocolate syrup

Directions

1. Combine all the ingredients in a bowl until smooth.

2. Pour the batter into the prepared baking pan.

3. Bake for 10–15 minutes.

4. Serve once cooled.

Serving Suggestion: Serve with milk.

Variation Tip: Use butter instead of margarine.

Nutritional Information per Serving:

Calories 127 | Fat 12.g | Sodium 23mg | Carbs 28.2g | Fiber 0.6g | Sugar 20g | Protein 1.2g

Chocolate Milk Brownies

Prep Time: 20 minutes

Cook Time: 15 minutes

Serves: 2

Ingredients

- 4 tablespoons flour
- 2 tablespoons milk
- 4 teaspoons sugar
- 4 teaspoons chocolate milk mix
- 2½ teaspoons shortening
- 2 pinches baking soda
- 1 dash salt

For the glaze:

- 6 teaspoons icing sugar
- 2 teaspoons chocolate milk mix
- 1 teaspoon milk

Directions

1. Mix all the listed ingredients (except the glaze ingredients) together in a bowl until well combined.

2. Pour the batter into the prepared baking pan.

3. Bake for 15 minutes.

4. Meanwhile, mix all the glaze ingredients together in a bowl until smooth.

5. When the brownie is done, let it cool slightly, and then spread the glaze over the top.

6. Let it stand for 2 minutes.

7. Cut into wedges and enjoy.

Serving Suggestion: Serve with ice cream.

Variation Tip: None, this recipe is easy and delicious!

Nutritional Information per Serving:

Calories 307 | Fat 5.8g | Sodium 311mg | Carbs 61g | Fiber 1.6g | Sugar 47.6g | Protein 2.1g

Granola Bars

Prep Time: 12 minutes

Cook Time: 10 minutes

Serves: 3

Ingredients

- ¼ cup rolled oats
- 3 tablespoons all-purpose flour
- ⅛ teaspoon baking soda
- ⅛ teaspoon vanilla extract
- 2 teaspoons butter, softened
- 1 teaspoon packed brown sugar
- 1 teaspoon mini semi-sweet chocolate chips
- 1 teaspoon raisins

Directions

1. Mix the rolled oats, all-purpose flour, baking soda, vanilla extract, butter, and sugar in a bowl.

2. Fold in the chocolate chips and raisins. Combine well.

3. Press the mixture into the prepared baking pan.

4. Bake for 10 minutes.

5. Let the bar cool for 10 minutes before cutting it into squares.

6. Enjoy!

Serving Suggestion: Serve the bars with some honey drizzled on top.

Variation Tip: Use baking powder instead of baking soda.

Nutritional Information per Serving:

Calories 168 | Fat 9.7g | Sodium 113mg | Carbs 18.1g | Fiber 1.1g | Sugar 6.9g | Protein 2.2g

Chocolate Coconut Bars

Prep Time: 10 minutes

Cook Time: 10 minutes

Serves: 2

Ingredients

- ¼ cup rolled oats
- 6 tablespoons coconut flour
- ⅛ teaspoon baking soda
- ⅛ teaspoon vanilla extract
- 2 teaspoons margarine, softened
- 1 teaspoon white sugar
- 1 teaspoon brown sugar
- 1 teaspoon semi-sweet mini chocolate chips
- 2 teaspoons coconut flakes

Directions

1. Mix the rolled oats, coconut flour, baking soda, vanilla extract, margarine, brown sugar, and white sugar in a bowl.

2. Fold in the chocolate chips and coconut flakes. Combine.

3. Press the mixture into the prepared baking pan.

4. Bake for 8 minutes.

5. Let the bar cool for 10 minutes before cutting it into squares.

6. Enjoy!

Serving Suggestion: Serve with milk.

Variation Tip: None, these bars are yummy just as they are!

Nutritional Information per Serving:

Calories 297| Fat 12.6g | Sodium 221mg | Carbs 37g | Fiber 16.3g | Sugar 8.9g | Protein 8g

Chocolate Peanut Butter Bar

Prep Time: 10 minutes

Cook Time: 4 minutes

Serves: 2

Ingredients

- 2 tablespoons peanut butter
- 4 graham crackers
- ⅓ cup mini chocolate chips

Directions

1. Place the graham crackers on the prepared baking pan.

2. Spread a thin layer of peanut butter on each of the graham crackers.

3. Top each cracker with some mini chocolate chips.

4. Bake for 4 minutes.

5. Remove and cool.

Serving Suggestion: Serve with flavored milk.

Variation Tip: Use dark, milk, or white chocolate chips.

Nutritional Information per Serving:

Calories 382 | Fat 19.9g | Sodium 353mg | Carbs 47.7g | Fiber 2.7g | Sugar 20.1g | Protein 7.9g

Oatmeal Fruit Bar

Prep Time: 10 minutes

Cook Time: 20 minutes

Serves: 2

Ingredients

- 1 tablespoon shortening
- 4 teaspoons brown sugar
- Pinch of salt
- $\frac{1}{3}$ cup flour
- 4 tablespoons milk
- $\frac{1}{6}$ teaspoon baking soda
- 3 tablespoons quick-cook rolled oats
- 3 teaspoons apple sauce

Directions

1. Combine the shortening, sugar, and salt in a bowl.

2. Add the baking soda, oats, salt, milk, and flour

3. Mix well to form a soft dough.

4. Place half of the mixture in the prepared baking pan.

5. Press down on the mixture in the pan with the back of a spoon.

6. Spread with 2 teaspoons of the apple sauce.

7. Place the rest of the mixture on top and press down.

8. Spread the remaining apple sauce on top.

9. Bake for about 20 minutes.

10. Once cooked, allow it to cool completely.

Serving Suggestion: When cooled, cut into slices and serve.

Variation Tip: Use butter instead of shortening.

Nutritional Information per Serving:

Calories 201 | Fat 7.7g | Sodium 198mg | Carbs 28.2g | Fiber 1.4g | Sugar 7.7g | Protein 4.2g

Fudge Brownies

Prep Time: 10 minutes

Cook Time: 15 minutes

Serves: 1

Ingredients

- 4 teaspoons flour
- 4 teaspoons sugar
- 2 teaspoons cocoa powder
- 1 tablespoon water
- 2 teaspoons oil
- ½ teaspoon vanilla

Directions

1. Mix all the ingredients in a bowl. Combine well.
2. Pour the batter into the prepared baking pan.
3. Bake for 15 minutes.
4. Allow to cool, cut into squares and serve.

Serving Suggestion: Serve the brownies with a drizzle of syrup and a scoop of vanilla ice cream.

Variation Tip: Use butter instead of oil.

Nutritional Information per Serving:

Calories 192 | Fat 9.6g | Sodium 2mg | Carbs 26g | Fiber 1.4g | Sugar 16.4g | Protein 1.7g

Peanut Butter Butterscotch Brownie

Prep Time: 12 minutes

Cook Time: 20 minutes

Serves: 2

Ingredients

- 3 tablespoons butter
- 2 teaspoons brown sugar
- ½ cup flour
- 1 teaspoon baking powder
- ½ teaspoon vanilla extract
- 2 tablespoons peanut butter
- 6 tablespoons mini butterscotch chips

Directions

1. Cream the butter and sugar in a bowl.

2. Mix the flour and baking powder in a separate bowl. Add the butter mixture to it. Combine well.

3. Add the peanut butter and vanilla. Mix well.

4. Add the mini butterscotch chips. Mix well.

5. Pour the batter into the prepared baking pan.

6. Bake for 20 minutes.

7. Allow to cool and then serve.

Serving Suggestion: Serve with a drizzle of caramel syrup.

Variation Tip: Use baking soda instead of baking powder.

Nutritional Information per Serving:

Calories 617 | Fat 37.6g | Sodium 305mg | Carbs 58g | Fiber 1.9g | Sugar 31.6g | Protein 10.4g

Lasagna

Prep Time: 10 minutes

Cook Time: 15 minutes

Serves: 2

Ingredients

- 4 ounces lasagna, cooked
- 1 cup ricotta cheese, shredded
- ½ cup mozzarella cheese, shredded
- 1 egg
- 1 serving spaghetti sauce

Directions

1. Whisk the ricotta, mozzarella, and egg together.

2. Place one layer of cooked lasagna on the prepared baking pan.

3. Spread some of the cheese mixture on top.

4. Place another layer of lasagna on top, and then some more cheese mixture. Keep layering until all the ingredients are used up, or the max line of the pan is filled. You may need to cook in batches.

5. Pour over the spaghetti sauce and bake for 15 minutes.

Serving Suggestion: Serve with a salad.

Variation Tip: Use a combination of your favorite cheeses.

Nutritional Information per Serving:

Calories 312 | Fat 9.3g | Sodium 575mg | Carbs 38g | Fiber 0.2g | Sugar 0.4g | Protein 18.8g

Cheesy Bagel

Prep Time: 10 minutes

Cook Time: 5 minutes

Serves: 1

Ingredients

- 2 slices deli ham

- 1 bagel, cut in half, toasted

- 6 tablespoons processed cheese, softened

Directions

1. Put one ham slice on top of a bagel half.

2. Put two tablespoons of cheese in an oven-safe cup and cook it for 3 to 4 minutes to get a smooth texture.

3. Drizzle the warm cheese on top of the ham.

4. Cover the bagel with another half.

5. Enjoy.

Serving Suggestion: Serve with milk.

Variation Tip: Use your favorite kind of cheese.

Nutritional Information per Serving:

Calories 477 | Fat 23.7g | Sodium 2187mg | Carbs 40g | Fiber 2g | Sugar 8.8g | Protein 30g

Cheese and Pepperoni Muffins

Prep Time: 10 minutes

Cook Time: 20 minutes

Serves: 6

Ingredients

- 1 English muffin, split
- 2 tablespoons spaghetti sauce
- ¼ cup mozzarella cheese, shredded

Toppings:

- 1 tablespoon pepperoni, diced
- 1 tablespoon mushroom, diced
- 1 tablespoon onion, diced

Directions

1. Place each half of the muffin in the prepared baking pan.

2. Add the spaghetti sauce and then the toppings on top of each half.

3. Top each half with the cheese.

4. Bake for 15–20 minutes.

5. Enjoy!

Serving Suggestion: Serve with milk.

Variation Tip: Use your favorite type of cheese.

Nutritional Information per Serving:

Calories 290 | Fat 12.3g | Sodium 695mg | Carbs 35.5g | Fiber 1.2g | Sugar 2.1g | Protein 11.7g

Apple Pie

Prep Time: 10 minutes

Cook Time: 30 minutes

Serves: 1

Ingredients

- $\frac{1}{3}$ cup pie crust mix
- 4 teaspoons water
- 6 teaspoons pie filling, apple

Directions

1. Mix the pie crust mix and water together in a bowl with a fork.

2. Divide the dough into 2 balls.

3. Roll out one of the balls on a floured surface. Cut it to fit into the base and slightly over the sides of the prepared baking pan.

4. Put it into the baking pan and fill it with the apple filling.

5. Roll out the second dough ball. Place it over the top of the filling. Seal the edges.

6. Bake for 30 minutes.

Serving Suggestion: Serve with a dusting of powdered sugar.

Variation Tip: You can add some cinnamon for flavor.

Nutritional Information per Serving:

Calories 328 | Fat 18.3g | Sodium 432mg | Carbs 37.4g | Fiber 0.4g | Sugar 6g | Protein 4g

Blueberry Pie

Prep Time: 16 minutes

Cook Time: 30 minutes

Serves: 2

Ingredients

- $\frac{1}{3}$ cup pie crust mix
- 4 teaspoons water
- 6 teaspoons pie filling, blueberry

Directions

1. Mix the pie crust mix and water together in a bowl with a fork.

2. Divide the dough into 2 balls.

3. Roll out one of the balls on a floured surface. Cut it to fit into the base and slightly over the sides of the prepared baking pan.

4. Put it into the baking pan and fill it with the blueberry filling.

5. Roll out the second dough ball. Place it over the top of the filling. Seal the edges.

6. Bake for 30 minutes.

Serving Suggestion: Serve with flavored milk.

Variation Tip: None—it's delicious as it is!

Nutritional Information per Serving:

Calories 413 | Fat 7.1g | Sodium 211mg | Carbs 86g | Fiber 3g | Sugar 54g | Protein 1.4 g

Cherry Pie

Prep Time: 10 minutes

Cook Time: 30 minutes

Serves: 6

Ingredients

- ¼ cup pie crust mix
- 2 teaspoons water
- 4 teaspoons pie filling, cherry

Directions

1. Mix the pie crust mix and water together in a bowl with a fork.

2. Divide the dough into 2 balls.

3. Roll out one of the balls on a floured surface. Cut it to fit into the base and slightly over the sides of the prepared baking pan.

4. Put it into the baking pan and fill it with the cherry filling.

5. Roll out the second dough ball. Place it over the top of the filling. Seal the edges.

6. Bake for 30 minutes.

Serving Suggestion: Serve with milk.

Variation Tip: None, it's perfect as it is!

Nutritional Information per Serving:

Calories 305 | Fat 17.8g | Sodium 430mg | Carbs 32.3g | Fiber 0g | Sugar 1.3g | Protein 3.9g

Banana Split

Prep Time: 10 minutes
Cook Time: 20 minutes
Serves: 1
Ingredients

- 1 packet sugar cookie dough
- 2 tablespoons banana, sliced
- 2 tablespoons strawberries, sliced
- 2 tablespoons pineapple, drained
- 2 tablespoons seedless grapes, halved

Directions

1. Put the cookie dough in the prepared baking pan and press down.
2. Bake for 20 minutes.
3. Let it cool on a rack, and then place the fruit on top.
4. Refrigerate for2 hours and then serve.

Serving Suggestion: Serve with a whipped cream topping and some toasted almonds.
Variation Tip: Use any kind of fruit you like.
Nutritional Information per Serving:

Calories 210 | Fat 9.2g | Sodium 101mg | Carbs 32.3g | Fiber 1.2g | Sugar 19.1g | Protein 2.5g

Cheese Sauce/Dip

Prep Time: 10 minutes
Cook Time: 5 minutes
Serves: 1
Ingredients

- 4 teaspoons soft cheddar cheese spread
- 1 teaspoon water

Directions

1. Mix the cheese and water in a bowl.
2. Place in the baking pan.
3. Let it melt in the oven, about 5 minutes (but keep an eye on it!).

Serving Suggestion: Serve with nachos.
Variation Tip: You can add some seasonings if you prefer.
Nutritional Information per Serving:

Calories 200 | Fat 16g | Sodium 380mg | Carbs 4g | Fiber 0g | Sugar 0g | Protein 12g

Asian Peanut Sauce

Prep Time: 10 minutes

Cook Time: 9 minutes

Serves: 2

Ingredients

- 2 tablespoons smooth peanut butter
- 1 tablespoon soy sauce
- 1½ tablespoons pineapple juice

For dipping:

- 2 carrots, sliced
- 2 apples, sliced

Directions

1. Mix the peanut butter, soy sauce, and pineapple sauce in a bowl.

2. Place in the baking pan and warm it up in the oven, about 9 minutes.

3. Let it cool and use it as a dip.

4. Enjoy!

Serving Suggestion: Serve with the sliced carrots and apples.

Variation Tip: None!

Nutritional Information per Serving:

Calories 243 | Fat 8.5g | Sodium 569mg | Carbs 41g | Fiber 7.9g | Sugar 28.6g | Protein 5.6g

Beef and Tater Tot Casserole

Prep Time: 10 minutes

Cook Time: 30 minutes

Serves: 1

Ingredients

- ½ onion, diced
- ½ pound ground beef
- 5 ounces cream of broccoli soup
- 2 ounces cheese soup
- 4 ounces cream of mushroom soup
- Pinch of garlic powder
- Pinch of Italian seasoning
- ½ cup frozen vegetables, diced
- $\frac{1}{3}$ cup cheddar cheese, shredded, plus more
- Salt and freshly ground black pepper, to taste
- Tater tots, as needed
- 1 teaspoon butter

Directions

1. Heat the butter in a saucepan. Add the onions and cook for 5 minutes.

2. Add the ground beef and cook for 10 minutes.

3. Mix the soups, vegetables, garlic powder, Italian seasoning, cheese, black pepper, and salt in a saucepan.

4. Add the ground beef and onion to the soup mixture. Mix well.

5. Carefully place some of the mixture into the baking pan. Be careful not to overfill. Place the remaining mixture into an airtight container and refrigerate to use later. It will keep for up to 5 days (longer if frozen).

6. Put some tater tots on top and sprinkle with more cheese.

7. Bake for 30 minutes.

8. Serve and enjoy.

Serving Suggestion: Serve it hot.

Variation Tip: None; this recipe is delicious as it is.

Nutritional Information per Serving:

Calories 1028 | Fat 48.2g | Sodium 1775mg | Carbs 77.9g | Fiber 9.3g | Sugar 4.7g | Protein 69.5g

Cheese Pizza

Prep Time: 15 minutes

Cook Time: 20 minutes

Serves: 2

Ingredients

- 3 tablespoons all-purpose flour
- $\frac{1}{6}$ teaspoon baking powder
- Pinch of salt
- 1 teaspoon butter
- 2½ teaspoons milk
- 1 tablespoon pizza sauce
- 1½ tablespoons mozzarella cheese, shredded

Directions

1. Mix the baking powder, flour, salt, and butter in a bowl.

2. Add the milk and keep stirring.

3. Combine the mixture into a dough and place it in the prepared baking pan.

4. Use clean fingers to pat the dough over the bottom of the pan, then pat it up the sides.

5. Pour the pizza sauce evenly over the dough.

6. Sprinkle with the mozzarella cheese.

7. Bake for 20 minutes.

8. Serve.

Serving Suggestion: Serve with chopped fresh basil on top.

Variation Tip: Use parmesan cheese instead of mozzarella cheese.

Nutritional Information per Serving:

Calories 127 | Fat 6g | Sodium 251mg | Carbs 11.1g | Fiber 0.5g | Sugar 0.6g | Protein 7.6g

Cheese Quesadilla

Prep Time: 5 minutes

Cook Time: 5 minutes

Serves: 1

Ingredients

- 1 small tortilla

- 1 cup cheddar cheese, shredded

Directions

1. Cut the tortilla into wedges small enough to fit inside the baking pan.

2. Sandwich the cheese between two wedges.

3. Bake for 5 minutes or until the cheese melts.

4. Once done, serve.

Serving Suggestion: Serve with your favorite toppings.

Variation Tip: Use mozzarella cheese instead.

Nutritional Information per Serving:

Calories 508 | Fat 38.1g |Sodium 713mg | Carbs 12.2g | Fiber 1.5g | Sugar 0.8g | Protein 29.5g

Caramel Apple Tart

Prep Time: 10 minutes

Cook Time: 20 minutes

Serves: 2

Ingredients

- 4 teaspoons sweetened condensed milk
- 1 teaspoon egg yolk
- 2 teaspoons apple juice
- 1 packet sugar cookie mix
- 6 tablespoons of whipped topping
- ¼ apple, cut into small slices

Directions

1. Whisk the egg yolk in a bowl and add the apple juice and condensed milk.

2. Add the sugar cookie mix. Mix well.

3. Pour the mixture into the prepared baking pan.

4. Bake for 15 minutes.

5. Take it out and let it cool completely.

6. Apply the whipped cream and garnish it with the apple slices.

7. Enjoy.

Serving Suggestion: Serve with vanilla ice cream and caramel syrup.

Variation Tip: You can add a pinch of cinnamon.

Nutritional Information per Serving:

Calories 276 | Fat 7.6g | Sodium 91mg | Carbs 50.5g | Fiber 1.1g | Sugar 0.4g | Protein 2.7g

Conclusion

Making kid-friendly, easy, delicious baked recipes is simple and fun with the Easy-Bake Ultimate Oven! This oven provides kids with the freedom to enjoy baking in their homes, learning all about ingredients and their preparation. They can enjoy hours of fun creating anything from cookies to cakes to snacks.

Your kids will love this cooking guide. We have presented more than 100 recipes in this book, with beautiful pictures and snippets of nutritional information. It also incorporates some essential tips and tricks to kick start their cooking journey.

We hope you have as much fun making these recipes as we did creating them. Happy baking!